PRAISE FOR

DOMESTIREXIA

"*DOMESTIREXIA* is an astonishing pleasure dome of lyric cake, all verve and scrumptious compression."
—GREG WRENN, author of *Mothership: A Memoir of Wonder and Crisis* and *Centaur*

"Poems that wriggle and teem with life and its sense data— razored down to eerie, tilting monuments by Novak's exacting art." —NOAH WARREN, author of *The Complete Stories* and *The Destroyer in the Glass*

"Novak's voice makes material out of her linguistic virtuosity, and makes it look easy."
—BEN FAMA, author of *DEATHWISH* and *FANTASY*

"I think of Sylvia Plath listening to Joanna Newsom while assembling a bouquet in Wonderland. This is an exquisite and rare collection of poetry that feels magically out of time."
—CLAIRE DONATO, author of *Kind Mirrors, Ugly Ghosts*

"*DOMESTIREXIA* is abuzz with alarm, charm, and excess. It's scintillating, a swarm."
—CASS DONISH, author of *The Year of the Femme*

"Novak makes language feel alive and peculiar, defamil-iarized and zoolike."
—ARISA WHITE, author of *Who's Your Daddy?*

"Novak's poetic mirror shows how the consumptive tedium of domesticity can double for an ornate tomb."
—SADIE DUPUIS, author of *Cry Perfume*

ALSO BY JOANNA NOVAK

DOM EST IRE XIA

poems

JoAnna Novak

Soft Skull New York

First Soft Skull edition: 2024

Library of Congress Cataloging-in-Publication Data
Names: Novak, JoAnna, author.
Title: Domestirexia : poems / JoAnna Novak.
Description: First Soft Skull edition. | New York : Soft Skull, 2024.
Identifiers: LCCN 2024011288 | ISBN 9781593767631 (trade paperback) |
ISBN 9781593767648 (ebook)
Subjects: LCGFT: Poetry.
Classification: LCC PS3614.O9264 D66 2024 | DDC 811/.6—
dc23/eng/20240312
LC record available at https://lccn.loc.gov/2024011288

Cover design by Jaya Miceli
Cover images: flower and animal crackers © Shutterstock;
abstract city narrow light © Getty Images / Cheryl Molnar
Book design by tracy danes

Published by Soft Skull Press
New York, NY
www.softskull.com

Printed in the United States of America
1 3 5 7 9 10 8 6 4 2

Contents

i.

Dear Ornamental

I take the compliment
to my second self

in the garden,
white vinegar breath

an axil from her lips.
Learning how

a strong stake aids
a slender, unassailable

stalk is a matter of denial
and solace. I want

appurtenances of accepting
the compliment

more than I can mother
another hour.

Patience, patience,
O despotic little nodes!

My second self counts
BBs, nigella seeds, sugar ants,

defending her right
words: bulbils.

Demanding a future
like the compliment,

black, focused, a hope
light as a petiole,

cardamom, clove.
My second spans,

fingers surrender
in E-Major cashmere

gloves. French Suite.
And me, grave? Of course.

I serve all my guests tiger lilies.

Dear Unfeeling Martinis

Bless you,
stomach pump.

Bless you,
puce hole.

Bless you,
balcony

and cool
air that finds me

éthylique
on the floor

pushing in
the broken door.

I open it
and hate it

with equal
slosh.

Just wetting the
cork,

bless it.
Shorn

plum buds
pruned

from Thai basil
in Italian terracotta.

I do miss
traveling

with my poison
pen, loving

this cocktail,
lying about

would-be
devils, demons-

trating my vile
behaviors, all

excessed
and how

feckless
I used to

behave
bowing,

boiling,
baring

my voluptuous
shoulders.

Dear Aries

He began by parching me,
      reserving the cup

for oracles. If I could
      ward off famine

with signs, let them be
      ram in the sky,

hard-nosed. Humped.
      I coughed up cartilage,

crept to the wood,
      this Joey can do better—

I knew I could—
      I will. Show him

my grip, reared
      to wring the stars

from his silk.
      See him Taurus

there, crouching, Krios
    unwinged,

bedding me golden,
    razing my fleece.

Good Game

I plan to play for hours, a day, a week,
maybe, entertain myself, whatever

—there goes a lifetime. Confronted with
that box, I like it every way.

I pull out pieces and let them move.
The cards, I muss, face down, up, overdo

plugs and battery panels, confuse jacks for
dice in the half-light. I use a thick fist

where my palm is sufficient, and of course I
like to bruise. Better still, I bet for blue.

My coming is sure and after a while we
are all the same. Hot. Abused.

I forget that, and you, too. I hide my hand and
find a strange orange cut, an organ

of loudness and fuss. Tallies, scores? I
ruse them. Sometimes I cheat,

but to cheat at solitaire is dazzling
regression. Slide a thumbnail through

the plastic, cue the beer lamp. I keep cups
in the cold, almonds in oil. I promise; I crush;

I, hopeful. I plan to accept the holidays, give parties to
others, and me, a walk-the-dog joy

—toy, unshareable toy. I prepare fingerprints
for the fridge. In this very door, I have a skeleton key.

ii.

Abundance

and olives and oranges
and dye and a pattern
and win, win-win,
praying verdure
prying the missal
joy, this raiment,
and alms and almonds
patina ballerina
green table, chair pair

***

***

German novella, Jewish novelist
four-way stop, off-leash dog
cayenne and grapefruit
aves and vespers
a ring from two mothers and
gold to sell
and gold to share
I sought time enough
and sleep to spare

***

***

and milk overnight
milk filled the ghosts
and drenched the linen
sweet and stormbule
flight and a fast
the riches of home
and coffees and cures
birds and whatever
and les arbres so resilient

***

***

this boy in my arms
his head in my palm
little lip sweetsucked
brown mango, soft brie a
dream, holy day
I showed him the
kittens
in Texas a drama
weaned for mon fils

***

***

an urn and a plot steak
and champagne red
wine, cocoa butter
cakes for $14,000
a clutch and a kitchen
Dutch oven, springform
back issues, back bedroom
lily-trotter, lovebird
lemons overwhelming

***

***

I couldn't believe this
cardinal hopping
red fluff
in the yard
and more, green
all day long, the spread
of history, goodness,
the morning
made me hungry,
unstable, and talky

***

***

spinach and scallions
stars and star anise
apricot aquafaba and
Italian meringue
pistachio paste
and feuilletine
fists finger-full
fudge in a pot,
copper handle heavy

***

***

a cake for Monet
a cake for Bosch
a cake for Dali
cake for Seurat
cake O'Keefe
cake Cassatt
shaped like
their favorite animals
in the dictionary

***

***

this perishable world
crusty vowels, silent regions
in a dream I spun
left and shot
the man in his bottle-
cap nose, vigilante
minus a halo
what are the keys?
where are toothpicks?

***

***

with pleasure or
praise
we deserve
leeks
and little gems
honorable
invitation *meet*
me
in the pantry

***

***

making much of little
ribbon brisket
knish gnocchi
rubber carrot,
latex bone
I chalked
the rabbet day
O Dei, sick present
coughing blood carnations

***

***

and patent purse and patent pumps and
patent father, patience paddleboats
and rowing long
and RC Cola anchors
and zipper pulls
and peanut butter
zippy scissors
in a dream
I made the past de novo

***

***

here I am hatched
heaven and a hole
latticed with luck
drowsy and blowing
how should I have known
to be ecstatic and obvious
unration the rules
better tomorrow
I save the fate of sugar

***

iii.

A Girl and Her Egg

I was already blindfolded, a walking diary—
distracted, stuck, inspirited and on top of them, him and
her and, ici, les personnes. Yet I steadied my
forearms, and the black rabbit composed a path from
arbor vitae to awning.

Gold morning. Or yellow lights on an old truck,
buying everyone's new springtime.

"The desire, if it's kept alive, will often be validated
with an idea," he whispered in my mouth. Two
obsessional seconds he held me underwater. Mr.
Grey-Cat cinched the sash and scoured the skillet
and set the droplets skittling. I bled my eye.

The kisses I'll remember: Molten. Set white on uova
in purgatorio. Bullseye yolk smeared on bit lip.
Misophonia, stolen from nest.

"Get sleep and a little bit of food," he said. Such a
senator! He put me in the lilac fridge, no towel, one
slipper. I was his heaven, still learning to speak.

Workaroundish

Off I go, he said.

Must, must, must have miso, she said.

I want everyone to do what I'm doing, he said.

I'm not trying to scare myself, but, she said.

Are you scared? he said.

I'm trying, she said.

For better and worse, this is the paradigm I see things through, he said.

Leave your phone in the car, she said.

Kiss peace goodbye, he said.

I remember now, she said.

I texted you the recipe, he said. No capers, use anchovies.

I remember now, she said.

My dad is eating in the garage, he said.

Now you and him—, she said.

I didn't have those models, he said.

Forcefield, she said.

Howitzer, he said.

Forcefield of intimacy, she said.

His no-hugging business, he said.

Suburban cowboy, you could call it, she said.

That wall came together in two days, he said.

Is it hard for you to see him like this, my mother said,
she said.

Covers for the pontoon, he said. The radio through
the wall.

I know, she said. I remember.

Country music—he said.

I'm sick of talking about my family, she said.

Arrest is inevitable, he said. I'm telling you, he said.

I feel so selfish, she said.

We could probably pay it off in five years, he said.

Do you want to know my three-year plan? she said.

My mother, he said.

My mother, she said.

She wants to be treated like a child, he said.

Without, she said.

The fulcrum, he said.

A tool shaped like a carrot, she said.

Your father, he said.

A fork in the water, she said.

Meet us at the water tower, he said.

I haven't showered, she said. My hair—

—, he said.

Just my little exercises, she said.

Lots of sources. Psychiatry Today, he said.

Stop, she said.

You're the most paranoid person I know, not by a little, he said.

One second, she said.

He's no nonsense, he said.

Nauseous, she said.

Nauseated, he said.

That's vomit on my shirt, she said.

Seventeenth-century, he said.

There's never been a study, he said.

I'm not the one, she said.

Djinn, she said.

I wouldn't, he said.

I don't want to, she said.

I don't want to cook, he said.

I can't, she said.

Forget it, he said.

The bone uncurling, she said.

Hock, he said.

I'm nauseous, she said.

A big fleshy worm, she said.

Nauseated, he said.

Can you? she said.

She's at the top of my list, he said.

White miso, she said. White miso caramel.

Belover

He says nothing to the garlic. Mother Mayhem is in
the kitchen. Gutter water tugs the door, cracked from
a wayward sun. And the cat dragging his bum leg.
The cat called Patience. Of farm and ficus.

If only the son could be mastic. Chromaticism,
chromosomes, clutched undercover. He turned a
knob and the flame was sidereal.

Are you attracted to me? He asked the onions. Huh?
Huh?

Meanwhile, she kneaded her temples. He was
mauling the beef, massaging the marble,
applaudable marbling—it's Charity, Mother.
Patience and Charity mewl in the alley.

Stop worrying.

Well, grow up. She'll worry if she wants.
You don't tell me what to do, Mr. Blue Battleship Tattoo.
You'll see nail heads on the floor.

Nothing to Lose

She looks fondly at the firedogs, their vague ashen
fur. Upstairs, his suitcase gasping. Fifteen days, the
same snookered towel stank on the music stand,
where he displayed Father Fickle's sketches.

Ma-ahm—look, MAH-m!

Two chicken tenders on flour tortillas, that fishy
blankness as he fills a Budweiser bowl with ice water.
Sometimes, she can't shake the père from the fils, red
and white and bootblack all over.

Be only a girl: What other rule is there?

She is still sweet, one dove in a bowl of milk. She is
poking a palmier or watching a livestream of eaglets
divide a squirrel, feet stretched out by the fire. She
conjugates kindly: *I speak, I used to speak, I spoke.*

A Kind Living Room

Yes, be capable of kindling oneself; no, absolutely,
not. Have pride in ineptitudes—book untouched.

Some album sits on a shelf. Negatives long as sticks
of gum. She said he said they say don't touch leave
our fingerprints we might need that muck that's the key
to reprinting the picture. History—so abricoté.

Another morning, just another shitty morning, Grown
Gamma says, lean in her gauzy gown.

With fear, with feelings, with an open door, she is
inside the Oldsmobile, radio wired to the precinct
dispatch all those Fridays faking sick to copilot for
her tolerant father.

Son frères, son péres. 'sa shame.

He explained the pains of boys, outside Otto's. The
stein on the sign was the color of breading.

Spikenard and Sprat

The beauty of the breast at two, at four, at seven, at
ten, at two—small hand reining her hair—sharp nails
scratching her throat—inside, outside, against the
trellis, below the well—sure grip fisting Mother
Mayhem's mouth—chrism in the basement, dimness
over-seen by three eras of fish, plank-mounted—
encaustic gills, razor fins, blessed maw and gaze—

Quit, she said, 40xs, do something you love—story
nested in every family, the floundering nuclear; thank
you for holding the baby—a truth oiled and won,
walking to a waterfall, they spoke—joy spread, so
fleecy and dull—cul-de-sac, underpass, bridges—
looking fondly at each other—breath hitched in
gray—a date, another day—

when they returned bacon burned, Al Green, their
baby sated in his highchair.

Highboy

I think today of corners, how they allot space, and last
night my head was lower than soap on the drain. I
think today of corners, and last night I thought of
you. You taught me to hide. To hide to hear to sneak
down, duck the cellar door. Gold is stable; so am I.

From the dormer in the nursery, I watch Cheerful
Chuck reroute a spout. He is focused, tongue
knotted in his cheek like a hickory nut. Cheerful
Chuck caulks his cocoa-brown stripes, good gutters are
wide gutters, he says, $1569, fair price.

A slow accrual of wealth under a stratum of dying
magnolias. The rules of dividends crack sidewalks,
slanting the historic district.

What if simplicity saves nothing? If my
monochrome chant is a red grunt? Spine like a
scythe, I'm naked under this surplice, picking
varnish off my palms:

bad razor + bad blade = rufous stigmata.

I love your sense. I love your stability. I love your
advice. I love your father making furniture, joints
joists vices files ferries roses and fathers, were I a

man I'd be a father, shan't I, shouldn't I, someday: I
know nothing, I am trying to learn. I am not a
novena, prayerfully blank, embittered esposa, easily
drunk, painting foxes, teeth in denial, on tall chests of
drawers. Let me survive the hand-me-downs and
sentiment, the flinch before savings. Do I look
vegan? Slow-mo flamboyant? What can I do?

Come here, come stay, come over. Bring your
sloppy dog, your stormy windbreaker, your animal
crackers, your scarab script. It's no way to live. I
want to drive all over the country, too, look beyond the
furniture. I spent decades multi-hearsed by the market,
you told me, don't do that. I have a spare bedroom.
As many as four coffins.

I heard the dresser topple at midnight. I nested till
morning. Up again, I was surrounded by dark hills
and gutters. Everyone went to Pert 'n Pretti.

What do you see, brown bear? What do you see,
purple cat? What do you need, black sheep?

Genoise with Mallow Rose

She liked sharing sweets with men, penance for
being a tart. Her lemon bars, or—Modish Marge's
bake. Sa sœur, too swazy for all that. Couldn't skim
solids off melted butter, couldn't gentle a sponge.
She smoked, got her grille, stacked Dayton's bills.
She died with two-dollar notes in one hundred bras.

He believed her: she was his mattress girl at
Rosedale; said she was pregnant. Not like she ever
came plain. Girdle, garter, gash; balconette,
bluebella, racerback; strapless mold, feather-lace
bralette. Never a nipple gal, but she did have a good
biscuit—malmseyed to the hilt, it went to her head.

Red hair, red lipstick, apron, gaga for church. In her
heart she believed. There were several true wounds. She
kept going, guzzling, folding flour into air.

, and as It Ought to Be

The floating hospital is leavened. And I am its
aproned mistress. Where bandages were, bread is
ordinary. Levain. Mother. Bialy. Bagel. Bostock,
brioche, biscuit. I am still not sure what decadence
I'm after, but I board and scoff at the wharf, holding
my French pin. Others are rinsing curtains. Others are
scrubbing shutters. Together we are the gale in an
ordinary machine. The rain cleans and spring birds
build nests in the girders. Tell me to get off the boat,
I'll bury my nose in a cookbook. Check.
Fasting agreed with me, made me limpid and
vigilant, a laminated dough, I could stay up for
hours, overnights, limewashed, laboring, and loyal.
Whence before I could barely spell adolescence,
whence before I was ravenous, yet advanced along the
plank and called it a path. "The more do I find work
a necessity," I read, "the greatest of pleasures."

iv.

Knife with Oral Greed

The barefoot
heroine, white
wax on her front
teeth, drags the
book across the rug.

What to make
of the predator,
with his pantry
of silk and silver
tesserae—

Looking bright red
in the snow,
the barefoot heroine stoops
to recall (allegedly
knowing nothing of Spain):

She got a chill,
seeing the cuchillo,
part of disenchanting a
mother-in-law
in a barrel of oil.

"I'm not so young anymore," she told the little cottage, on display and edited.

Exactly the number
of nights, foam
in a tub, tucked under her
apron, tender young
thing.

Twelve white flowers
and poisonous snakes
the barefoot heroine
ate with her wine
and cakes.

Standing on flypaper,
curling her piglet
toes, sighing—
that peach
leo.

The smell of
sweet jam
meant the tailor
slew her suitors,
ironed her stays.

She stitched up the
drawer before
leaving, testing the
road
between her legs.

Sheer good fortune
said the eggshell
with the fishnets,
in once upon a
midnight denier.

And she put her hand
in his pocket,
could see, boss-
eyed, his belt.
Greetings, comrade!

Fasten my buckle, turtledoves,
beg my thicket,
my hazel branch,
my coveteers.

To plunge
in the garden,
the barefoot heroine
squeezed a bee, gold
on the hasp.

With barely an hour,
she still stoops
and pecks beads from
the wigs, contentedly
chewing.

Thinking teething
is only embroidery.
Seeing an escort
at breast.
Needle on nipple.

This was a brown bear
gone to fat, dancing well
into dawn.
Let her
stomp on his paws.

Fur under sole.
Ashes.
Foreign king.
Filigreed MP3.
Staggering new year.

She sees crinoline
glass more than
window. Embarrassed by
the hiccoughing gifts
of her pink cup.

Then it's lunch, for skinks
in the underground palace. I
won't be so young
tomorrow, she spells
in petals and powder.

V.

As It Is . . .

Now briefly notice the health of the roof, its 700-
grade and decadent declivity, Italian clay tiles flounced
like a thousand taffeta skirts, peacock green and
slipped off beside the bed, confused as it is confining,
crowded together, sickness and health, under strict
guard. The true nature of the roof is one of heft and
durability, a roof that will pour off rain and melt down
snow and generally hold the home in plentitude while
you trot the globe and soap off rings, trace windows
and kiss strangers, share an apocalypse of strawberries
Romanoff. Comment upon the roof's viability is
unnecessary. The body has been touched and cleansed,
examined without hindrance. Forthwith declared
genuine, a folly of most extravagant complications: a
lady's hand doorknocker. Famed langues de chat
calves.

Hide the House in the House

Cannonade of dresser drawers, shut, shut, shut, shut.
Meet the Amá of Adjectives. O, calm, o canary horse,
canary horse sing, sing-a-sing-sing to pretty boy's
ears, dimple small as a tear.

Puzzle piece tipped with Paris green. Wool blanket
pulled to burning eyes. Bottomless cellar, sortie,
kiss. Their son versus their sleep? Their son's ears are
hers.

A game: study seventeen loud semesters and scatter the
card catalog. Add twenty-six inches and fourteen-
point-one-five pounds. Crinkle the summer plaid
swimsuits. Row the hot dogs, ketchup a moat.

Open, poppyseed.

What could they let go?

Whaling Wife, _____ Fife. The bruise provides a
secret room, very _____ and quite _____.

Sure as her semaphoring breasts, he is content. A
puzzle piece slitting the shrink wrap. Mr. You Only
Want to Judge. Mr. You Hate Other People. Mr.
Son Latched to Canary. Fix it. Go on. Weak seal on
the fridge, freezer of granivorous beaks.

"Water the Flowers You Want to Grow"

Nous avons le fougasse. Nous avons le chien et
nous avons le chat. Nous avons la chouette et nous
avons le cheval. Nous avons oui. Nous avons non.
Nous avons beacoup. Nous avons le mort. Nous
avons le lait, l'orange, la pizza, le chocolat. Nous
avons le cinéma. Nous avons le livre. Nous avons la
musique. Nous avons la voiture et le valise. Nous
avons le bain. Nous avons la famille. Le fils et le
pére et la femme. Nous avons le maison. Nous
avons le jardin.

Chinn's

Hurricanes come in commemorative cups, shy
lemon-lime. She would kill for the kids—that's why.

A phase of your forties: four AMs and wind suits,
engineering fasts. Sweats. In a den, in a drawer,
among metal rulers and metal-capped pencils, solve
for X and Y.

Accept it: her regular, low-grade discontent. Ration
animal crackers. Go out, don bib, hit rum. Crabs
and lobsters and the rolls, oh lord, rolls in garlic
butter, table tongs.

How many hurricanes in forty years? She likes
beer—that's new. He taught two children the
transitive property: Wristbands and racquetball.
Reebok tongues. She never learned how to be
happy. He remembers so much

working a cigar. Tomorrow, he'll hack the ping-
pong table; now he sits on the porch, watching the sky
for thunderheads.

Drizzle

When it stops, the chiffchaff, a gooseberry stain,
lightning in the trees. It has never needed a crown,
striped nor chevroned. When it stops, passerine
pause, our lips. Slip a prayer, locket a pill, link
hands. And joy jumps the baby boy's face. When it
stops, he thumps louder. Two legs, round toes. We
fold up the changing pad for another century.
Chuffing, stopping, stalling—doesn't it feel like
summer? we ask. It stopped, so we robed in silver
linings. Driveway drizzled brown of cardboard,
patter of parking lots we pass on the path, I-spying
through sedges. Here, two hundred cars six spaces
apart. Absurd. Relentless. The worms bunch and
cowl. Pew of the chiffchaff's perch, parish of
onomatopoeia. So active, so small a bird, so proud,
olive, its camouflage breast.

Little Things

She frosted her face like a naked cake. Stalwart
Scarlet, Mistress Mayhem, whatever-whatever, she
copycatted her eyes ermine. Toasted flour in a
skillet, sploshed milk.

"Show me proof, Painboy," she said. "Show me."

When she couldn't stop cooking, she went out. She
rode the unexpected rain, a slick mirror of morning, a
stern mirror of morning: minor hazy, gray-lipped,
lakeless.

Ration Modeling: Easter

Maple cream candy, peanut honeycomb—nougat,
nudge him from the floor—spending like so what,
still my mother's daughter, green pepper and cottage
cheese on rye—you did this to her—chicken and
Brawny.

These people, perfect for each other—their
mornings, their noises, rouse the dogs from their
cages, mug lost to the microwave—*for seconds the
sound did not reach them*—he likes spiral cut, she'd
rather ham off the bone—*this*, for $135?

He cradled the box—little shoppe—more expensive,
just like other chocolate—something to do, some
busy to keep—and a doctor knew her better than he
did—was it indulgent of me?—she journaled the date
twenty times, he worked through a weekend.

Bliss: cashflow and graphs and a map. *Ponderosa.* I
mean, we like having chocolate—one box in the
freezer, we could pace ourselves.

Ordinary life, family life, what else?—I think you
suggest make brownies at some point?

Todd at the Cemetery

I will buy the roses, I will bring the plate. Paten, said
Holy Hunk. What's Vatican for $600? What is
vestments for middle school? Two children, a
brother and a sister, see their clogs, brown and
peeking out from flaxen robes, rope belting their
natural waists. Butterick, Simplicity, Vogue pattern
books. A temperate Wednesday, March, ninety-five
days overdone, and the priest regaled her with every last
inch of Cartageña. Cusco canceled for summer.

*

She missed old everyday seasons: girlhood. Never
thought of her children as children—they were adults,
and there was herself. Her epaulets, her coxcomb
cap, her baton. Good Guy standing behind her in the
kitchen, flicking the crown of her head. There's a
bug on your bun, hun. She pressed her cheek to the
wall, the wood stained white, *Jeopardy!*. Don't
move.

*

Roses, roses, the nuns braided roses, folding petals
into beads. A backlog of rosaries bodes well, doesn't it,
Todd? The decaf beside the catalogue of urns.
He wore frosted frames. She looked awful, she could
tell.

But imagining herself, girl of twelve, girl of eighty, hair, pixie, bob. She runs a hand along the railing in the hallway, where she would plié all day. Plié, plié, relavé. Her mother died with good curls, good coverage. Her son at the deathbed said, Grandma, you've always had such beautiful hair. Mother—, she said, placing a beetle in her mouth.

*

Where will we be in twenty days? She hears herself taunt Todd at the cemetery. I don't know. Ready to bury my mother, that's for sure. He rings a bell on the desk and a blast of rosewater scents the room. He blinks prayerfully, whispers: *The moment is easy.*

*

Someone went to Russia. She was gifted like most girls. The nesting dolls were light as pinewood derby cars, minus pennies. Pennies are interest, a clown told her once. Light as balsa, borscht blush, kerchiefs half-covering their craniotomy lines. Bug in your brain.

*

Days of the week panties don't come in my size. Sunday, roses. Monday, roses. Tuesday, roses. Wednesday, Prince Spaghetti—lord, she loves saying *CREAMETTE.*

*

Her mother did not want to be in the ground. Her
mother did not want to be directly in the ground. Her
mother is in half an urn, the half not occupied by her
father. The urn in a box, the roses on the plate, the
plate tied to the box with a strip of burlap.
Todd. Ladybug ceiling, silverfish grout, stag beetle
with railroad ties, aphids in roses.

*

Thursday, Friday, Saturday, 1962, 1963, Monopoly in
the rocks and a screaming pink suit. Where were you
when you heard the news? Holding the edge of the
tub, homilizing, squeezing Mother Misery's
handsome hand: *Moses supposes his toes are roses
and Moses supposes erroneously.* Squinting out the
eye of a needle. Splinter in her palm.

Winkle-pickers

They speak of stones, hands sandy, cradling skulls of
rock. They fix their eyes shoalward. They hold still,
fearful and patient, snowbound on a Friday in April.
And they believe for a moment it is May.

Speak of the fall, after a summer of learning at
home. Less than houses: one raised room, one corner
bed, a cramped lamp table, a vent's rainbow grate.
Voices blow up, stewy warden, Mr. Headstrong cubing
    bloody meat.

Dewlap, they chant. Water parsley, be our miniature
four-leaf clovers. They are lucky, they are fed, they
have pockets to fill and access to Rice Lake. The
mussel broth is chatting with good sausage.

Count the times I interfered, the points I argued, the
truth I mistook for freedom. For surrender. Only
vanity is not me. Look for dark, banded shells. The
operculum. All safe underwater.

simon-pure

The dog peers under the blinds, previewing opera.
She has worn a dress in Vietnam, the dress of her
photogenic ancestor, a circus spaniel washed in lace
light, talon toes dusted with talc. Whose wife? It's
me, Second Fiddle, says la fille. Twists the dog's ruff
round her wrist and waits on a watch to appear.
Minutes, seconds, she is half-houred and certain she
sheaved sanity in the folio. A modest request, ten
miles in writing. Don't step slipper outside. You'll
get a letter—the dog is that wistful she missed the
storm.

Northwoods Paradise

The doctor wore blue, a Spanish heart—we don't
call them *atrophied* anymore, he said, speculum
ratcheting.

Wink, wink, ahem. A hem is a lip is a paper heart.

Of Great-Aunt Quincunx's nine cracked teacups,
only one leaks. Upside-down ballgown skirts: these
are the driest wells of love.

I needed something other than staring on the
couch, so I scraped flour from dead dough. I
dripped wishes from the ceiling.

I drove into another state with a plan called SKY
CHAIR.

All these years, I type, and finally give out. How
much longer will anyone like French?

Je veux.

Acknowledgments

Thank you to Mensah Demary for making a home for this manuscript at a press I've admired since I realized there were presses to admire. Thank you to Wah-Ming Chang, tracy danes, Rachel Fershleiser, Megan Fishmann, Cecilia Flores, Lena Moses-Schmitt, and the entire Soft Skull team for ceaselessly championing the literary arts. Thank you to Markus Hoffmann for shepherding my work across genres and for your counsel and friendship. Thank you to Claire Donato, Cass Donish, Sadie Dupuis, Ben Fama, Adrienne Raphel, Noah Warren, Arisa White, and Greg Wrenn for your endorsement.

Thank you to Kate Durbin and Eileen G'Sell for being early readers of this manuscript—you made it better. Thank you to Bradford Morrow, Rob McClennan, William Waltz, Susan Lewis, Dinah Cox, Remi Recchia, Allyn Bernkopf, and the *pulpmouth* team for giving these poems early shelter. Thank you to my teachers, here and gone, who guide me when I write: Glen, Monica, Kerri, Peter, Dara. Thank you to my colleagues and my students. Thank you to the institutions that provided fiscal support during this writing.

Thank you to my grandparents, whose house was my earliest home. Thank you to my parents and my sister. Pat and Martha, for offering shelter and stories during the first weeks of the pandemic, giving me space to read and write. Gary, thank you for *The Seven Habits of Highly Successful People* and every good conversation. Mac, nothing would've been possible without your presence and care during those years—my gratitude is forever. T, for modeling what it is to live beside poetry. N, for delighting in sound and letters and words, for making it contagious.

Publication Acknowledgments

"Dear Ornamental," "Dear Unfeeling Martinis," and "Dear Aries" first appeared in *Conjunctions*.

"Knife with Oral Greed," in a slightly different form, was published as a chapbook by above/ground press.

"Belover" first appeared in *pulpmouth*.

"Nothing to Lose" and "A Kind Living Room" first appeared in *Touch the Donkey*.

"Spikenard and Sprat" first appeared in *Dusie*.

"Workaroundish" first appeared in *Conduit*.

"Highboy" and ", and as It Ought to Be" first appeared in *Posit*.

"Good Game" first appeared in *Cimarron Review*.

JOANNA NOVAK is the author of the memoir *Contradiction Days: An Artist on the Verge of Motherhood.* Her short story collection, *Meaningful Work,* won the Ronald Sukenick Innovative Fiction Contest and was published by FC2. She is also the author of the novel *I Must Have You* and three books of poetry: *New Life*; *Abeyance, North America*; and *Noirmania.* Her work has appeared in *The New Yorker, The Paris Review, The New York Times, The Atlantic,* and other publications.